MW01171063

Revised Edition

BEAUTIFY YOUR LIFE FROM WITHIN

by Miranda L Moss

JULY 21, 2016

Atlanta, GA

ACKNOWLEDGMENTS

Creator of all things, I have more confidence in you than I do in myself. Provide wisdom to all who read from this book. Shine the light and begin the healing in women who seek the truth about who they are in Christ Jesus. Show them the knowledge of your will for them each day and give them the strength to carry it out. I give you the glory for this message. It's not my will but your will be done, in Jesus' name. Amen.

DEDICATION

This book is dedicated to the following women. Many of you have seen me go through different phases. Some were good; some were painful to watch I know. Thank you for giving me room to grow and for continuing to love me through the journey. I love you and may God bless you all.

My mother, Dorothy Moss, is the first to show me what it means to be a strong woman. My sisters, Yolanda Wheatley and Towanda Moss, always know what to say and keep it real. My *big sis* from another mother, Mrs. Brenda "Hello Gorgeous" Alford shines beautifully from within; her testimony blesses me. My other mother, Mrs. Jackie Clayborn, author of the cookbook, "Sweets by the Bay," inspires me to keep the faith and supports me in all of my endeavors. And Dr. Jean Hudley, founder and CEO of *Boys2Men Home & Sanctuary for Youth, Inc.*, it was nothing short of a miracle that we met. You are my mentor, my mama,

4

my friend. I marvel at your faith, your strength, and your passion.

INTRODUCTION

Beau-ti-fy, (verb): improve the appearance of, tidy up, revamp.

I felt ugly. I was fat and I didn't have good hair. My hair was so nappy- just short, dry, hard. It was never soft enough to slick the "baby hair" on the side of my face with hair grease. I never thought I could ever be pretty. No one ever told me I was. They told me that I was a smart girl. They said I was a quiet girl. And when someone wanted to be mean, I was called a fat girl. So I never knew there was anything attractive about me. Of course, I hated my hair. I hated being fat. Afraid of rejection, I didn't make an effort to make friends. I didn't like who I was and I wanted to change that. I became aware of all of this by the time I was ten years old. I didn't understand the loneliness I felt. But, I was always trying to avoid people. I wanted to hear a genuine compliment telling me I was someone special. I got tired of people making fun of me.

More than anything, I couldn't stand for anyone to bring up the subject of hair.

I remember sitting in the choir stand one Sunday; my family lived in Flint, MI at the time. Sitting behind me was a skinny, light skinned girl with long, wavy hair. She asked me, "Why isn't your hair like your sister's?" I froze. The question caught me off guard. My younger sister had long hair with soft curls framing her forehead and temples. People always stopped to tell her how pretty she was. So I was scared to answer the girl in the choir who had never said one word to me before. I don't know why I even responded. But I lied about having a hair disease that made my hair fall out. Her reply was, "What does that have to do with all them bb's on the back of your neck?" I heard girls and boys snickering behind me. I could hardly hold back the tears welling up in my eyes. I was so embarrassed.

From that day on, I was at odds with myself. I wanted to feel differently, look differently and think differently about myself. I couldn't. I believed other kids had better features than me and were more likeable. More than that, I was stuck on the opinions of other people. Their insensitive remarks defined me. I didn't know there was more to me than that. I believed I had problems. I even minimized my good traits. I didn't believe I was as smart as others said. I didn't believe I was as good or as sweet as others said. I accepted that only good looking people got attention. Talkative and bold girls seemed to have more friends, lived a happier life. By the time I was a teenager, I wanted someone to call me beautiful. I looked for someone to tell me that I was special. No one paid me any attention. I clearly didn't belong anywhere I wanted to be. I hated the life I lived and I began to constantly consider how to change it from the outside. Nothing I did externally ever made me feel good about myself for long.

This book discusses the value of self-acceptance. It gives girls and women the guidance to discover their best features and to learn that true beauty develops from within. My book presents women with an opportunity to search for spiritual awareness and personal growth by reflecting on their God-given qualities. These qualities are not defined by health, wealth, dress size or hair texture. Reflect on what is meaningful to you and savor it. While you read this book, I pray you will discover something so exciting and inviting about yourself that you will instantly make up your mind to transform how you think. I'm frequently aware of how beautiful my life is because of how I now think and feel about myself. You have to try it for yourself. Now is the time to validate yourself. Rejuvenate your mind. Elevate your spirit. Beautify your life from within.

By Faith and Love,
Miranda Lorraine Moss

BEAUTIFY FROM WITHIN

Makeover your mind
Never mind your face
Put down that blush
Brush on a little faith.

Beautify from within
With your self-reflection
Think of self-respecting
Not complexion perfection.

No substitutions
For warmth and honesty
No other solutions
For grace and modesty.

Beautify from within
Foundation of peace
Don't spread it too thin
Serenity smells sweet.

Thankfulness shapes your core
On days you don't feel your best
Bow down at heaven's door
Let God handle the rest.

Honor the gifts God's given
To beautify from within
You were never a blemish
Your radiance never dims.

"Don't be concerned about the outward beauty of fancy hairstyles, expensive jewelry, or beautiful clothes. You should clothe yourselves instead with the beauty that comes from within, the unfading beauty of a gentle and quiet spirit, which is so precious to God." 1 Peter 3:3-4 (NLT)

TRUE BEAUTY

We are beautiful women. I know we are beautiful because there is something about each one of us that is unique. Each one of us has an amazing quality. We are beautiful because we are fearfully and wonderfully made by God. God made no mistake when he created us. He gave us the spirit and the desire to be in reverent awe of his glory because of who he is. We are God's greatest masterpiece!

We were sculpted by holy hands. There is nothing simple, worthless or cheap about any of us. There's no cosmetic or clothes we can wear that turns our physical appearance into true beauty. We can't see true beauty by looking at our faces in the mirror. We need to look beyond what we can see with our own eyes. Our best

features are our innermost qualities-
intelligence, purpose, and spirituality.

*"For you created my inmost [sic] being;
you knit me together in my mother's
womb. I praise you because I am
fearfully and wonderfully made; your
works are wonderful, I know that full
well." Psalms 139:13-14 (NIV)*

INTELLIGENCE

Women are complex and interesting.
That makes us naturally attractive.
Just thinking about our talents and
skills, makes us sparkle from the
inside out. We know we've got it

going on. Despite our self-confidence, we want to hear someone else say how special, or how beautiful we are.

Many of us look for others to validate us. Therefore, we interact with people who can neither relate to our enthusiasm for life, nor recognize our God given gifts. We rely on family and friends to tell us who we are. My dear, listen to your heart. Those questions we silently ask will be answered in due time. Watch and pray. Everything we do is a reflection of what we think about ourselves. The quality of our relationships, the level of our education, and the occupation we choose reflects on our sense of self-awareness. We have to figure out who we are, right? Beloved, we must do what it takes to develop a sense of pride in the woman we are becoming.

We are on a journey with no destination. Our journey reveals a constant state of *growing*. Intelligent women don't know everything nor are they smarter than everyone else. Being intelligent can be as simple as knowing who we are in Jesus Christ and knowing how to live on purpose. We are thoughtful and resourceful. We are motivators. The depth of our self-reflection measures how well we monitor our thoughts and feelings. Our self-esteem makes us capable of negotiating life's obstacles. We must nurture self-love and invest in wisdom to be the woman we always wanted to be.

Wisdom Wake-up Call

As intelligent as I was, I made many foolish decisions to have sex with anyone who would have me. I wasn't very selective. I acted desperate. I acted out of a need to love and to be loved because I didn't love myself. I tried my best to fit into social circles willing to be anything or anyone except myself. That trend started in college and continued beyond my military career. I can't explain why I continued to let men use me and abuse me for years. It was killing me emotionally, but I couldn't help myself. I never wanted to talk about it because I had had enough being blamed and judged as a teenager. I didn't know anything except that I wanted a husband. I believed getting married and raising a family would make my life better. I got a wisdom wake-up call in my mid-forties. I was so fed up with my life, I wanted to kill myself. After nearly 30 years, I had come to recognize my pattern of self-destructing behavior. I finally admitted that I was addicted to drugs, alcohol, and I lived with a man who physically and verbally abused me. But, I was afraid to change. I didn't believe I could live a better life. How was I going to live without getting high? Who was going to love me? I was smart enough to know I could pray for help. Change didn't happen instantly. I rebelled some, but I didn't give up on myself. Eventually, I began to make better choices. I made an intelligent decision to know and to love Miranda.

Making poor choices is part of growing up. But, it's how we live in the wake of shame, blame, remorse

and regret that makes us overcomers.
Acknowledging our mistakes gives us
the power to overcome them. We can
turn our flaws and weaknesses into
strengths. We have the aptitude to
change our course when obstacles
appear.

Be strong-willed and self-assured.
Avoid dream stealers and joy killers!
When we blame everything else on
why we can't soar and reach our
greatest potential, we are thinking
like a victim. Victims are powerless
and make excuses about why they are

'less than.' Their favorite words are 'I can't.' We can own our potential by embracing who we are right where we are. Girls are supposed to grow up to be intelligent, self-respecting women. Maturing women should learn from their mistakes and experiences, both good and bad. Life is a great teacher if we pay attention to its lessons. We can't allow looks, location, family, friends, financial, or social status to validate our worth. Don't you know how powerful and gifted you are? We have IT. Want to be smarter? Learn to love self!

"And we know that in all things God works for the good of those who love him, who have been called according to his purpose." Romans 8:28 (NIV)

PURPOSE

As women, we must discover what we are created to do. We must embrace the purpose for which we are made. If we don't seek meaningful vocations that make solid career choices, we subject ourselves to allow

others to make choices for us.
Aimless living is no life at all.

Many times we make decisions that we later find were wrong for us. Through what can only be described as God's will, life just seems to make sense in the midst of the chaos we create because of self-gratification. If we are honest, we must admit that we think of ourselves far more than we should. Brutally selfish with blinders on is the best way to describe me years ago. Despite our worst efforts, our journey takes us to the most amazing places and we will never know how we arrived. God is, and that is all we need to know.

Wisdom Wake-up Call

Remember when I said I just wanted to get married and have children? I'm glad I didn't get what I thought I wanted. Initially, I only pursued education and worked jobs because that was expected of me. Striving to be a wife and mother was no exception. I never knew what I wanted in life. For nearly 50 years, I didn't know who I was. It wasn't that long ago the word purpose became part of my vocabulary. I asked myself these questions for years: Why am I here? What am I supposed to do with my life? I always loved to read and write. Someone suggested I write a book. She thought I had an interesting life. Me? Interesting? Writing a book about my life proved to be more difficult than I thought. So I put it off to write other things. I became a writing consultant to help others develop their writing skills. I made a part time job of proofreading and editing. I wrote poetry, resumes, term papers, book reviews, newsletters, reports, etc. My wisdom wake-up call gave me insight into what path I was created to take. My purpose isn't crystal clear to me yet. Just knowing I'm headed in the right direction gives my journey momentum. One summer I volunteered to tutor adults through a non-profit organization. It dawned on me that I love to teach reading! Teaching incorporates my two passions reading and writing. It suits my personality. I'm patient and accepting of others. My students are the most important thing to me and I love them. I want the best for them. I will not let them fail academically or in life. Not on my watch. My prayer for my students is that they become lifelong learners who are willing to share their knowledge with others. My goal is to be an effective and reliable reading teacher. I'm so excited and serious about that, I enrolled in graduate school to earn a

Master's degree in Reading and Literacy. When I look back over my career choices, this feels just right. Teaching reading feels like my purpose in life. Not because it's a career path, but because my community involvement gives my life meaning. I take learning seriously. I'm offended by a system that labels struggling readers as future convicts and turns its back on them.

Teaching others how to read is my way to help families succeed and improve the quality of their lives. To

God be the glory, my life was never about what I wanted.

God has placed something wonderful inside of all of us that is meant to serve a greater good. It's inspiring to find what it is we have that is too incredible to ignore. We must perform beyond the insensitive labels society puts on women—weaker sex, emotional, gold digger. The more we give of self, the more we will receive in return. What we get in return is mainly heartfelt. We can't be deceived by promises of fame and fortune. Seek truth, not easy answers. Settling for anything that looks good and sounds good will compromise our beliefs and stunt personal growth. Ladies, acquire wisdom about your purpose. Living a purpose filled life gives us vision and clarity to make the right moves. As we grow older, we should no longer act out of immaturity, selfishness, or lack of direction. In pursuit of purpose, be charitable and wise.

"Instead, let the Spirit renew your thoughts and attitudes. Put on your new

nature, created to be like God-truly righteous and holy." Ephesians 4:23-24 (NLT)

SPIRITUALITY

When I was growing up mama used to say to me and my sisters, "God don't like ugly and he ain't too particular about the cute." It basically means we shouldn't think too highly of ourselves. God doesn't show favoritism (Acts 10:34, NLV). So don't believe the hype. No one is highly favored by the Father. It's most important to have a reflective and humble demeanor. Having the right attitude and selfless motives keeps us spiritually in check.

A right or wrong attitude depends on how we respond to every situation. It's perfectly okay to express a variety of emotions- sadness, joy, anger, excitement. It comes natural to smile and feel good when things in our lives are working as they should. We laugh easily. We smile more readily. We may even treat others more favorably. The truth is no one has a perfect day every day. We get sick, disappointed, mistreated, abused, and we grieve what we lose. We are human. However, expressing any of those feelings for a prolonged period of time will begin to change how we typically talk to and treat other people.

In addition to checking our attitude, we can also maintain our spirituality by evaluating our motives. Beware, though, good intentions don't mean we always act selflessly or morally. We tend to overlook the red flags. Those warning signs steer us away from unintended mishaps. First, we get the feeling that something is wrong. Then, the Holy Spirit reminds us that we know the difference between right and wrong. We might call it wisdom, intuition, a hunch; we know what we know. Next, we are faced with choices. Incidentally, we talk ourselves into justifying our motives. But chances are, there is only one right answer. Let's evaluate our thinking! We must stop and consider the consequences. *What happened the last time? Do I have all the information I need? Does this feel right?* If instant gratification is the goal, better think again. Our idea of the perfect ending could change from a positive to a negative, from being harmless to dangerous, from requiring a sense of urgency to abort mission. Finally, after a careful assessment of risks and consequences, it's time to make a decision. We come to the proverbial crossroads. We can turn right, left or stay on the same path. We can go back to where we started. Or we can choose to stay put and make no decision. Most of us believe that our first thought is the best, the only or the right way to think. We must constantly check in with our heart and humbly ask *Am I doing this for the right reasons?* If we don't check our motives and redirect our thinking, we set ourselves up for problems. Our decisions bring pain into our lives. We inflict pain onto our loved ones. We let the devil use us in ways we never intended. Also, we stop praying for God's mercy and start panicking. We stop praising

God's grace and start pacing the floor. We stop seeking God's way and we start seeking worldly ways to fix our problems. Don't ignore the red flags!

Wisdom Wake-up Call

I've been emotionally detached for most of my life. I acted the way I saw my parents behave. Distant. Critical. Unapologetic. Growing up, I thought making good grades would please my parents. It was the only time they appeared to like anything about me. Eventually, I didn't care what they thought of me. I couldn't stand to be around either of them. Mom and dad were always cursing and beating on each other. So when they talked crazy, cursing at me, I got an attitude. I talked back and bucked at whatever they said. I didn't think they were qualified to tell me how to behave.

I looked for approval anywhere I could find it. My personality changed every time someone didn't give me what I thought I deserved. I could always find fault in others, but couldn't see my shortcomings. I never had many friends. I was desperate to be included somewhere, anywhere. I did whatever was necessary to be likeable and attractive. I drank alcohol, experimented with drugs and had unprotected sex. By the time I became an adult, I was miserable. I developed a low tolerance for carefree, happy people. I told myself that they weren't all of that. Their "attitude" made me reflect on what I thought was wrong with me. Or I thought they were fake. Sooner or later, I drifted away from certain people. They had gotten too close or I decided I didn't like them that well. I told myself I didn't need anybody; no one can relate to me.

The truth is I couldn't relate to myself. Who am I? I wanted to know. I hated looking in the mirror because of how I felt inside. Afraid to deal with the results of my stupid decisions, I couldn't face myself. I wanted to die. Who should I turn to for help? I didn't have any friends and I kept my distance from my family. I reasoned that people were the source of all of my pain. The problem was always the other person, never me. Eventually, through self-reflection and spiritual growth, I realized I was angry inside. I possessed self-hatred and fear. I always did what friends, family and men required me to do to be accepted. They thought they had me figured out. In hindsight, the root of my low self-esteem was my inability to validate myself. The wisdom wake-up call that checked my spirituality happened when I finally admitted to myself that I was angry and lonely. I didn't know if I was lonely because I was angry or angry because I was lonely. It didn't matter because I knew what had to be done. I knew that I had enough of feeling low, self-medicating with drugs and alcohol and living with an abusive man. I needed to change. I needed to beautify my life from within. I had some work to do. I began to get serious about my prayer life and trust what God created in me. I read the whole bible in a translation I understood. I made a note of the scriptures that rang a bell inside of me. I needed answers to a lifetime of questions. It took some soul searching to request professional help for coping skills. My faith in God led me to let go of my self-loathing lifestyle and let go of people I allowed to steal my joy. I love myself today. I do what makes me feel happy, loved and free.

Once we discover what we need to work on then, we must do the work. Here are some basic things we can do to get started.

<u>Think positively.</u> Consider it the bright side or the silver lining. Think of sunsets, butterflies, or the beach. Whatever we can think of to turn a bad mood into a better one, is positive thinking. We can chase away angry thoughts with the power of music. We know songs that will put us in the best mood and empower us. Let's replace negative words with inspiring

ones. Reading scriptures and poetry helps. Expressing our feelings in a journal allows us to look at our motives. It's also good to write down what makes us happy. Remember to take a step at a time, one day at a time. Bottom line is you don't want to feel pain, frustration or helplessness for very long. We have to get empowered to do something for self to raise our own spirits. When we have that positive vibe about us, we can give it to someone else who needs cheering up.

<u>Wear a fabulous smile.</u> We make others feel great when we form our facial features into a kind, pleased, and amused expression. That is our inner beauty shining through. There is nothing wrong with turning up the corners of our mouth and exposing our teeth. Why is smiling important? An expression of happiness is therapeutic. When we are feeling down, sick or moody we want to share our smile, our approval, our love for others. Smiling is contagious; someone will give it back to us. Trust

it. A happy face makes all the difference when we are having one of those days.

Express gratitude. Life doesn't come with a satisfaction guaranteed disclaimer. Nothing is more dissatisfying than searching for something that can't be found like contentment. Many will describe contentment as being happy, fulfilled or maybe grateful. Regardless of how one defines it, contentment doesn't come to us naturally; it can't be purchased, or manufactured. Learn to bc content because nothing is guaranteed to last forever. I'm talking about wealth, health, family and friends, just to name a few. There may be many reasons to feel unfulfilled, but isn't there so many more reasons to feel grateful? Be like the fearless child who finds life thoroughly amusing. Find contentment in simple things.

Live a God-centered life. Developing a spiritual life and Godly habits will last us a lifetime. Prayer, worship and meditation are the stepping stones to

51

living a God-centered life. Focus on what's beautiful, not what's wrong. Give compliments instead of criticism. Be good natured, not a gossiper. Like the old hymn suggests, "Build your hopes on things eternal. Hold to God's unchanging hand."

"For I am convinced that neither death nor life, neither angels nor demons, neither height nor depth, nor anything else in all creation, will be able to separate us from the love of God that is in Christ Jesus our Lord." Romans 8:38-39 (NIV)

THE COMPLETE PACKAGE

There isn't a diamond, ruby, pearl or
any other stone, gem, or metal as
precious and as priceless as we are.
Let's discover what makes us unique
individuals and hone those qualities.
Whether we are funny, happy,
studious, genuine, athletic, artsy,
musical, body-pierced, tattooed, long
haired or short, hairy or hairless, tall
or diminutive, curvy or petite…accept
that it's enough. Nothing else matters.
Celebrating who we are, showing
how amazing we are, knowing how
special we are is what makes us

exquisite. No one is meant to be the same as someone else all of the time. Even identical twins show different personality traits. We can represent our best qualities no matter how quirky we think they are.

We are interesting because we are creative and yet full of mystery. That's right. Be a mystery. Women don't hide, and yet we don't put everything about us on display. Let people who are worthy of us take the time to get to know us. If they are worthy, they are willing to allow us to get to know them as well. People we take time to know are kind to everyone, truthful, grateful, smart, and responsible. Now being creative can mean we are unpredictable, fun loving, carefree, inspiring, well-rounded. Using creativity means many, different things to different people. We learn who we are by trying out many, different things! Be full of life. Have fun. Being good-natured and grateful are the right attitudes to have. Knowing that we are truly loved is such a beautiful feeling! Love self. God loves us and there is nothing and no one that will change that, ever.

Wisdom Wake-up Call

God began to speak to me long before I made the decision to stop drinking, quit getting high, and to change my life around. I held onto the vision that I could change long before I believed in it. My wisdom wake-up call enlightened me about the woman I was to become. It happened over the course of a few months. I was unemployed one year.

I had no income, but I was getting high every day. I owned a home where I couldn't pay the mortgage on time, and the lights were off more than they were on. And I was going through a terrible time with my family. I was barely speaking to my parents and younger sister. I felt like they kept steering me towards pain and resentment again and again. I thought I would go crazy!! I couldn't breathe. Yet I would snort, smoke and sip on anything that would fog up my mind and dull the aching parts. My soul was crying out, my spirit drowning in self-hate and pity. This is what God did for me that summer: He put me on a cruise ship, then on an airplane and then on a mountain. I found myself in beautiful places as if I had money to even plan a trip! Everywhere I went, I was compelled to get on my face, bible open and pray, thanking God for something that I couldn't see or touch. It wasn't about my current destination. It was about where I was headed. You see, I couldn't get high and I wanted to more than anything. Isolating me was part of the Great Jehovah's plan (Hallelujah!!) The thought (His thought, His wisdom) that began to resonate with me was that my life was about to change radically. I had to be willing to change. By sending me on those trips, God showed me He was preparing places for me to go where drugs and alcohol will not be accessible to me. I would no longer want to associate myself with aimless, visionless people. I was leaving my comfort zone because God had a plan for me. I didn't even know what was to come. I could feel it stirring inside of me like I was pregnant with hope. That is why this book begins with a prayer. I'm so blessed to know how much God loves me!

As long as we continue to invest wisely into ourselves, we are becoming. We grow more valuable, interesting and loving. The journey is a beautifying experience. Being the complete package is knowing the qualities and opportunities that exist within. The complete package is taking the steps toward spiritual beauty based on Godly wisdom. The woman who is the complete package trusts in the process and delights in her work.

CONCLUSION

Self-acceptance is about identifying and declaring who we are by the choices we make. We can never be afraid to become who we are. Sometimes it takes willingness to begin the process to change our mind.

Other times require us to be honest with ourselves. Ultimately, it takes courage to live life differently from the way others live their life. Not everyone will understand how and why we beat the odds. Not everyone will understand our journey. Our spirit illuminates from the core of our soul. We are genuine. And we don't sacrifice our intelligence, purpose and spirituality. We are not victims. Ladies, we are overcomers. Accept the challenge to be amazing! Despite our past mistakes or our dress size, we have what it takes to accomplish greatness. Feeling beautiful is a choice. Let's always invest wisely into our mind and spirit. Let's make life a beautiful reflection of who we are within. Remember, we are truly a valuable, work of art.

OPPORTUNITY

You heard the knock
Now is the time
Like a new bulb
You're ready to shine

This is your year
Today is your day
What you call dreams
Keep you wide awake

You got the call
Prayed for a way
Never enough time
So just start today

Got to jump higher
Grab hold to that star
Got to work harder
To elevate that far

No one but you
can do what you do
What God has
He meant it for you
Sharpen your vision
around the clock

And long after
you've heard the knock

You heard them laugh
Now you laugh too
Better show them all
They can't get to you

Don't set them straight
Your family or friend
There's no heaven or
hell
They can put you in

Jump at the knock
Trample the floor
When it opens wide
Walk right through the
door

No one but you
can do what you do
What God has
He meant it for you
Chase your dreams
around the clock
And long after
you've heard the knock

64

LIFE BEAUTIFYING TIPS

Now that you know what you are made of, discover how to maintain it. Here are some tips to take with you on your journey.

PRAY

"Be joyful always; pray continually; give thanks in all circumstances, for this is God's will for you in Christ Jesus" 1 Thessalonians 5:16-18 (NIV)

Prayer changes things. Pray about everything. Pray constantly. Prayer is a stress reliever, pain killer, and sleep aid. Prayer energizes and calms. Praying brings us astounding peace.

MANAGE YOUR THOUGHTS

"Finally, brothers and sisters, whatever is true, whatever is noble, whatever is right, whatever is pure, whatever is lovely, whatever is admirable-if anything is excellent or praiseworthy-think about such things." Philippians 4:8 (NIV)

Cut out negative self-talk. If there is no one around to encourage us, we have to encourage our self. If there is no one present who believes in us, we have to believe in our self. Get knowledge and understanding. Don't be afraid to learn and ask questions. We can guard our heart by walking away from naysayers and gossiping people. Nothing good will come of keeping company with them. Always look for the good in others. Think positively and expect positive results.

BE YOURSELF

"But the fruit of the Spirit is love, joy, peace, patience, kindness, goodness, faithfulness, gentleness and self-control..." Galatians 5:22-23 (NIV)

Stay true to self. Don't change for anyone just to please them. We can make adjustments to our characters by trying new things, getting to know who we are. We want to be trustworthy and of sound character. Being a people pleaser will only give us painful results like resentment, abusive relationships, and negative self-talk.

GIVE

"Each man should give what he has decided in his heart to give, not reluctantly or under compulsion, for God loves a cheerful giver." 2 Corinthians 9:7 (NIV)

It is better to give. Learn how to compliment others. Be congratulatory and a motivator. Keep it positive.

Yes, we can present a smile even when we don't feel like it. When we encourage others, they often will encourage us too. Pitch in and help somebody. Don't always have a hand out to receive something. Give something back. Our lives will be immensely richer for the effort.

ABOUT THE AUTHOR

Miranda Moss teaches reading fluency and literacy strategies to students and adult learners. She began teaching professionally in early childhood education specializing in the care of young children from infants to three years old. From a young age, Ms. Moss has always had a passion for reading and writing. She is also a writing consultant who works with students, businesses, and aspiring writers. She is writing a series of books on spiritual awareness and personal growth. Ms. Moss is an air force veteran who loves traveling and animals. Ms. Moss currently lives in Lithia Springs, GA.

Made in the USA
Columbia, SC
15 October 2022

69471905R00039